Moritz Schuppert

A treatise on gun-shot

Written for and dedicated to the surgeons of the Confederate States Army

Moritz Schuppert

A treatise on gun-shot
Written for and dedicated to the surgeons of the Confederate States Army

ISBN/EAN: 9783337197032

Printed in Europe, USA, Canada, Australia, Japan

Cover: Foto ©ninafisch / pixelio.de

More available books at **www.hansebooks.com**

ON

GUN-SHOT WOUNDS:

WRITTEN FOR AND DEDICATED TO THE

Surgeons of the Confederate States Army,

BY

M. SCHUPPERT, M. D.,

Of New Orleans, Louisiana.

———

NEW ORLEANS:
PRINTED AT THE BULLETIN BOOK AND JOB OFFICE.
1861.

PREFACE.

We are in the midst of a Revolution in which Southern rights and Southern chivalry are arrayed against Northern aggression and Northern fanaticism. Large armies are rushing to the contest, and while preparing for the deadly struggle, all the appliances of modern warfare will be brought in requisition. We may, therefore, expect to see many a bloody battle, many a hard won field. The soldier is already dreaming of glory and renown, and, therefore, eagerly grasps the theories of war; but military tactics necessarily leave out of the question the ghastly field, its wounded, and the bed of suffering. There the province of the physician begins, and on the field of battle itself, his knowledge and skill are put to the severest test. He must be prepared and ready for every emergency; he has no time to consult, no time to read up, he must act; for while he hesitates, the current of life may be ebbing away. We have thought that a short manual on the treatment of gun-shot wounds might be serviceable at the present time, and though we admit that many are more competent for the task, none will undertake it with more zeal.

INTRODUCTION.

In the following pages we propose to present our readers with a brief and practical account of the treatment of gun-shot wounds. While omitting all theoretical discussions, we intend to explain principally the treatment of those gun-shot wounds which are complicated with injuries of the bones. Our views and treatment are based upon the experience of some of the most celebrated military surgeons of the age, and that experience is gained by a treatment of over two thousand shot-wounds, in the late war in Schleswig-Holstein.* Boldly may we assert, says Esmarch, that those three years' experience in the treatment of gun-shot wounds has established a new era in the history of military surgery. It is now settled beyond a doubt, that in future, amputations will not be deemed indispensable, and that, though primary resections of the shaft of bones are generally to be considered a dangerous enterprise, resections in joints are a new and great acquisition. More than three hundred doctors from all parts of Germany, have witnessed the favorable results chiefly obtained from resections of the elbow-joint. The prejudice of old military surgeons, who thought that resection of a joint was inadmissible during war, must now be done away with, for experience has shown that this operation was successful under circumstances where even amputation proved fatal.

---

* We have derived the greatest information in this respect from the invaluable writings of Stromeyer, Surgeon-in-Chief, and Esmarch, Physician to the Staff, in the army of Schleswig-Holstein.

TREATISE ON GUN-SHOT WOUNDS.

GENERAL OBSERVATIONS.--PROVISIONAL BANDAGES.-- TRANSPORTATION OF THE WOUNDED.--MANAGEMENT OF MILITARY HOSPITALS.

Capital operations are seldom executed on or near the battle field; yet it is well known that when amputation of an injured limb is indicated, every hour's delay diminishes the chance of the patient's recovery. In most cases the wounded are conveyed to the hospitals with a temporary bandage. It is here that we experience the most painful disappointments. Operations however skillfully executed, very seldom result favorably, notwithstanding the most careful after-treatment. The principal cause of this frightful mortality is mismanagement of the wounded on the field of action, together with the miserable conveyances on which the wounded are usually carried, sometimes over a distance of many miles to some hospital. Thus it is that a crushing of any one of the long bones is soon followed by the symptoms of concussion in the whole limb; all the cellular tissues around the wound, including the nerves and vessels, are covered with extravasated blood, sensitiveness is diminished from the shock and compression of the nerves, causing a kind of paralysis. The circulation in the veins is diminished, and this stasis of blood is soon followed by an abundant exudation of serum, infiltrating all the soft parts. The wounded are conveyed from the field of battle on badly constructed wagons, which cause them to suffer excruciating pain; the muscles of the injured limb become spasmodically contracted, so that the fragments of the splintered bone are driven into the flesh. We frequently find, moreover, that ill adjusted bandages increase the evil. From fear of hemorrhage, the surgeon applies a roller around the injured limb. This bandage being put on tightly, acts as a tourniquet, stops the circulation, but increases the serous exudation; should there happen to be a laceration of one of the larger blood-vessels, the bandage increases the danger, for the blood, though prevented from escaping externally, becomes infiltrated into the cellular tissue; the pressure and swelling which are thereby occasioned, being generally followed by gangrene of the whole extremity. The care, says Esmarch, with which the wounded were properly bandaged and conveyed from the battle field to the hospitals, was probably the means of bringing about the happy results which followed the subsequent treatment of many severe injuries, complicated with lesions of the bone, after the battle of Idstedt. The surgeon who accompanies the army on the field of battle has, therefore, great responsibility; for, upon his preliminary dressing much of the result of the after treatment depends. It ought to be his chief aim to support the wounded limb in such a way that the fragments of the bones cannot be displaced during transportation, and also, that the sufferer be made as comfortable as possible. For this purpose, a well applied bandage, with splints, resting on a pillow stuffed with finely cut straw or oat-chaff, will prove very serviceable.

In fractures of the humerus, the best bandage that can be used is a small cushion placed between the chest and the fractured limb, the latter of course being supported by a mitella (sling) and a roller around the body.

A fractured thigh should be placed in an abducted position and rotated outwards, supported on a large pillow filled with chaff, or placed on a double inclined plane. A fractured leg is best attended to by putting it in a fracture box, which consists of four boards—a bottom, two sides, and a foot board, joined by hinges, in such a way that they can close at right angles, and thus receive the wounded limb properly supported on a pillow.

A fractured forearm should be placed on a properly padded

splint, care being taken not to exercise undue pressure on the internal condyle.

The wagons used for transporting the wounded should have good springs. In default of these, moveable springs could easily be provided so as to be adapted to the interior of any wagon. On these springs a light frame work can rest, to receive a mattrass upon which the wounded can lie.

As soon as the wounded arrive at the hospital, it is the duty of the surgeon in attendance, to make at once a careful examination of the wounds. This examination is of the utmost importance, for it has to decide whether an operation is necessary or not. If the injury is found to be of such a nature that an attempt to save the limb would hazard the life of the patient, amputation must be performed at once. The advantage of immediate action is acknowledged by all military surgeons. On the other hand, in attempting to save the injured limb, great care should be taken to maintain a perfect adaptation of the fragments of bone together. The simplest apparatus are always the best. We have already mentioned cushions filled with oat-chaff as very advantageous in this respect. The surgeon should not leave the bed of his patient until he has placed him in such a position as to relieve him from all pain. Laborious and tiresome as this may be, the good results which the surgeon obtains, are, besides the thanks of the sufferer, sufficient compensation for the trouble.

Another important point in the treatment of the wounded, is the selection of proper places for the establishment of hospitals. Buildings should be well ventilated in order to prevent the development of miasma. Such localities, therefore, ought to be selected, which admit of a plentiful supply of fresh air. Unfortunately, it often happens after a battle, that the wounded must be placed in localities which are unfit for hospital purposes : still the surgeon can do much in such cases towards improving the condition of his patients by attention to ventilation. He should not fear a draft of air as much as a deficiency in this respect. The war of Schleswig-Holstein has proved that the best results were obtained in those localities where a permanent ventilation was instituted day and night.

As the surgeon will meet with prejudice from the wounded
and the nurses; it may become necessary to have the window-
shutters permanently removed, so that the regulations may be
certainly carried out. Cleanliness is of the utmost importance
in a hospital. In dressing the wounded, also, too much cleanliness cannot be used. The dressings soaked with pus and
blood should be taken out of the room immediately after
being removed from the patient. Sponges should not be used
at all, as it is impossible to keep a separate sponge for each
patient. The wounds should be first washed with warm water
poured out from a spout and afterward wiped with dry
charpie.

INJURIES TO THE SHAFT OF BONES.

THE NATURE OF THOSE INJURIES.

In a critical examination of gun-shot wounds of the long
bones, we must make a distinction between those which injure
the continuity or shaft of the bone, from those which implicate
the joints or the extremity of the bones. For injuries of the
joints involve more dangerous consequences than injuries in
the length of a bone. Before taking up this subject, however,
we shall say a word in regard to the injuries caused by
cannon-shot or bomb-shells. Wounds from such projectiles are
generally accompanied with extensive laceration of the soft
parts, or loss of the entire limb. Such wounds generally
prove fatal, on account of the shock to the nervous system;
death commonly taking place in the first twenty-four hours,
or mortification may ensue from which the patient dies usually
by the fourth day. The loss of an arm does not necessarily
prove fatal, but the danger increases with the proximity of the
injury to the trunk. For we often find simultaneous injuries
of internal organs, as for instance, rupture of the liver and
spleen. Not less dangerous are those injuries where extensive
fractures of the bones have taken place, though the soft parts
are uninjured. We diagnose the frightful extent of such injuries by the singular sensation derived from the crepitation of

the fragments of bone when we press upon the limb. Mortification here commonly ensues. The only chance of recovery in such cases is to amputate at once so as to save the wounded the pain of transportation, for this is certain death.

When a ball strikes the shaft of a bone at right angles, going through a limb, the bone is generally shivered into many fragments. The size and number of these splinters vary considerably, many of them being still connected with the soft parts. It is now well settled by a great number of observations, that these fragments retain their vitality, as long as the periosteum is not detached from the surrounding parts, and that they can be united by callus to their fragments.

Baudens, in his "Clinique des plaies d'armes à feu," adopts Dupuytren's classification of splinters into primary, secondary and tertiary, and recommends the extraction of all splinters, whether loose or still connected with the integuments; and he further advances the principle, that all bones should be resected as far as a fissure exists; but experience has proved that this precept is dangerous. Fissures, like splinters, may heal by the formation of callus. The older surgeons regarded fissures as very dangerous, an opinion which has some foundation, if inflammation and putrefaction should happen to supervene; for then necrosis will follow, unless the patient should succumb from phlebitis, a complication which is very frequent in wounds associated with fractured bones. The danger increases when the fissure extends into the joint. But, as in fractures of the bones of the skull, at least in young individuals, a fissure seldom extends beyond one bone, on account of the sutures, the same thing takes place in the long bones. There fissures of the shaft seldom reach the joint, neither will a ball passing through the epiphysis cause a fissure of the shaft. It is only when a ball happens to strike the exact point of union between these two parts, that a fissure may extend in both directions. The explanation of this fact is easily found, if we bear in mind that the shaft and extremities of bones are formed by separate points of ossification, and

2

may be shot off without fracturing the bone itself. These cases generally have a favorable result. On the other hand, a ball may penetrate the bone, remain in it or pass through it without the bone being fractured or splintered. Such cases, which occur mostly in the upper portion of the tibia, allow a favorable prognosis. Finally, a ball may strike a bone and become flattened against it, without causing a fracture. But those portions of the bone which are struck, generally mortify, for the periosteum is necessarily destroyed. Such cases, where one of the long bones has been so injured, when brought into over-crowded hospitals, are apt to cause suppuration of the medulla, and death commonly follows by purulent absorption.

EXAMINATION OF THE WOUNDS.

No task appears easier than to recognize an injury of a bone if accompanied by an external wound. For such injuries, it seems, could be more closely examined than simple un-complicated fractures; experience proves, nevertheless, that error occurs more often than the correct diagnosis. This can be explained by the abuse which the surgeons generally make of their probes, for they commonly use this instrument in their examination, though in reality nothing can be learned from it, whereas the finger is the best and most reliable probe. It would be well, says Stromeyer, if all the probes could be confiscated at the beginning of a war, for then surgeons would have to use their fingers instead. Another difficulty in the examination of gun-shot wounds arises from their very nature. Whereas in ordinary fractures the periosteum is generally separated with the bone, in gun-shot wounds the periosteum may remain entire, though the bone itself is fractured, so that the form and position of the bone remain apparently intact. This deception will occur even after a digital examination, if the limb be not examined in the same position in which it was when the injury occurred. The deeper the wound, the more difficult the diagnosis becomes. In this condition, if a doubt arises as to sacrificing or preserving the limb, and a digital

examination cannot settle the question, the surgeon should not
hesitate to make a free incision so as to increase the original
wound, in order to examine its exact condition.

PROGNOSIS.

There is no doubt that a gun-shot wound complicated with
an injury of the bone, is more dangerous than without it.
The gravity of the injury is proportioned to the size of the
bone, and the prognosis rendered more doubtful the nearer the
wound approaches the trunk. The condition of the soft parts,
which are generally lacerated by the fractured bone, exercise a
great influence upon the extent and gravity of the subsequent
inflammation. That the fracture itself does not aggravate the
case, is easily demonstrated by comparing the result of those
cases where only one bone was broken, with those in which
both were fractured. The former generally progress favorably
and the inflammation is circumscribed; but when the fragments
of the bone have been displaced by the action of the muscles,
keeping up a constant irritation, as occurs when both bones
are broken, then the most extensive inflammation will be
found. Another serious consideration in the prognosis of these
injuries is their tendency to pyæmia, a circumstance which
might be explained by the anatomical fact, that the veins of
bones are always open, having no power of contractility, and
therefore greatly favor the absorption of pus. It is of the
utmost importance to find means by which the medulla of a
long bone could be protected against purulent absorption.
Certain constitutions are not susceptible of pyæmic intoxica-
tion; nevertheless, many of these sink from the exhaustion
which accompanies an extensive suppurating wound.

TREATMENT.

A fresh wound is not aggravated by introducing the finger,
to ascertain the extent of the injury, or to remove foreign
substances, such as the ball or pieces of cloth together with
the fragments of bone which are detached. When it is re-

quircd to enlarge a wound it should be done in the line of
the long axis of the bone.

When the ball can be easily felt by the finger, a strong
forceps should be introduced, guided by the index finger of
the left hand, and as soon as the forceps touches the ball, the
finger is withdrawn, the ball seized with the forceps and
extracted. We must carefully abstain from too long a search
for a ball, and if it cannot be easily reached, or cut out on
the opposite side, it should be left untouched. Of all foreign
substances, a bullet is the most harmless, as proved by
numerous instances in which it has remained in the bones.
What is true of the ball, is also applicable to splinters.
Those which are entirely separated from the bone, should
alone be removed. It is remarkable, how frequtly fractures
heal after a small exfoliation of bone, when no attempt was
made to extract any splinter. This generally occurs, where
the ball having passed entirely through the limb, and where there
was no necessity to search for the projectile. Those splinters
which are still connected with the periosteum should be the
last removed ; even if the periosteum be separated from the
bone during the subsequent inflammatory process it will assist
in the formation of a new bone, whereas, in the beginning
a splinter could not be removed without carrying with it
the periosteum. On the principle above stated, remarks
Stromeyer, I consider extensive resections in the continuity
of bones inadmissible in recent wounds, because they cannot
be executed without simultaneous removal of the periosteum,
for then the ends of the bone are less apt to unite, than
when this membrane is intact. Besides this, a resection of
bone increases the liability of inflammation or suppuration.
I do not wish, however, to be understood as arguing against
sawing off the sharp and pointed fragments of bone, if it
can be done without enlarging the wound. All the cases in
which extensive resections were performed during the campaign invariably proved fatal. The precautions which are
necessary even for the extraction of foreign substances in
wounds of recent date, are still more necessary when the

opening made by the ball is so swollen, that the finger can hardly enter without causing the patient great pain. In such cases an examination ought only to be made when an operation is dependent upon the diagnosis. If there be any hope of preserving the limb, the wound should not be touched, either with the finger or probe. In fresh wounds an incision may be sometimes indicated, to get rid of a quantity of extravasated blood collected near the fracture, but after an interval of twenty-four hours, such an incision is entirely inadmissible, for it would allow the entrance of air to the collected blood, would cause it to decompose, and thereby prevent its absorption; it also increases inflammation and suppuration, and therefore the tendency to necrosis in the fractured ends of the bone. On the contrary, when inflammation can be subdued, we find that the splinters which are already loose will alone be separated, and only the ends of the fractured bones exfoliated. Knowing the obnoxious influence of a necrosed bone in retarding the healing process of a wound, it should be our greatest care to remove this source of irritation. But this is not always in the power of the surgeon. The great means of preventing inflammation and necrosis, are, *rest, antiphlogistic treatment, and free discharge of pus.* If the prognosis be favorable, and hope of preserving the injured limb be entertained, the attending surgeon should place the wounded extremity in such a manner that the fragments of bone cannot be displaced and irritate the surrounding muscles. Large cushions filled with chaff or chopped straw will be of the greatest advantage. If the extremity be shortened by a displacement of the ends of the fractured bone, no attempt should be made to overcome the deformity by any method of traction, for some time after the patient has been admitted into the hospital. The consequence of such an attempt would only produce fresh irritation of the soft parts without the end being accomplished. On the other hand, a few days' rest, under a proper treatment, will result in a relaxation of the muscles, and then the bones can be easily brought in a better position and retained there by splints. The treatment of wounds should be as simple as possible. The leading principle for the surgeon is to watch closely the condition of the wound, and remove all influences which interfere with the healing process. When wounded men were brought to the hospitals, says Esmarch, with the shafts of the long bones crushed by balls, if the limbs were already well bandaged and supported by splints on the field of battle, and the external appearance did not indicate infiltration or some other dangerous complication, we let them remain as they were. After placing the limb properly, cold applications were used, and no attempt made to remove splinters, or interfere with the wound in any other way. Under such a treatment we have seen cases recover in a short time, with very little suppuration, even where the thigh-bone itself was fractured. The wounded limb should be brought, if possible, into such a position, that it can be dressed without being moved. The greatest injury that can be done to a wounded limb in the beginning of the treatment, is to move it too often. The importance of keeping a wounded limb completely at rest, is unfortunately not so generally understood as it ought to be. This will spare the patient much pain, and avoid slight and repeated bleeding,—together with irritation which keeps up inflammation.

Another element in the proper management of gun-shot wounds, consists in an antiphlogistic treatment. That great man, John Hunter, says in his treatise on gun-shot wounds, that the injuries of the extremities did not bear blood-letting as well as injuries of the trunk. This doctrine is approved by most surgeons says Stromeyer, but, as I have already stated in relation to the treatment of simple fractures, I consider it erroneous, and have always seen the best results follow venesection in the treatment of complicated gun-shot wounds. But, alas! the value of blood-letting, is like so many other valuable remedies, now discredited, and expectant homœopathy seems to rule the day, so that young physicians are afraid to practice venesection. As they treat pneumonia, without blood-letting they think it just as reasonable to avoid venesection in traumatic injuries of the body. The small and contracted pulse, which is so commonly met with in recent gun-shot wounds, seems to forbid venesection, but in most cases such a pulse will be found to rise soon after blood-letting. The appropriate time for bleeding is within the first three days after the patient recovers from the first shock. If suppuration has taken place, venesection is no longer indicated, though leeches may still be sometimes used with advantage, when applied in the neighborhood of the fracture to diminish the inflammatory swelling ; they will dispense with incisions, which otherwise may be required. When suppuration sets in *slowly*, venesection may be performed even after the third day, with benefit to the patient.

Many surgeons are averse to blood-letting. in complicated fractures, because they fear to weaken the patient in anticipation of the suppurative process which commonly follows these injuries ; but these surgeons do not consider that suppuration will be diminished in proportion as the inflammatory process is shortened. I have seen several patients die delirious within four days, from injuries of the upper extremities, from too much inflammation, and I am convinced that blood-letting would have prevented it. Younger surgeons, therefore, should not be afraid of drawing blood ; and this was the practice of the English surgeons during the French war, a practice which we entirely approve. Although the type of disease of our times appears to be less inflammatory than thirty years ago, and although practical surgery is bound to profit by the lessons of internal pathology, we think, nevertheless, that a mechanical lesion, such as a gun-shot wound, must be treated on different principles than a case of pneumonia, pleurisy, or typhoid fever.

Next to blood letting, cold applications, the use of ice, cold irrigations are the most efficacious remedies. The principal action of these cold water applications is to keep down inflammation and prevent early suppuration. These means will also facilitate the absorption of much of the extravasated blood, between and near the fractured parts of bone. If no care be taken to diminish inflammation and suppuration, the extravasated blood is turned into pus; which, added to the swollen and inflamed parts will exercise an undue pressure upon the veins, and by interfering with the circulation of the blood, will cause a stagnation and serous infiltration of the whole limb. This condition is often a precursory symptom of phlebitis and death. It seldom occurs in hospitals where iced applications have been made early. In using cold applications, it is necessary to make them directly on the wound. Charpie and sticking plasters should be avoided, as they prevent a free discharge from the wound. Another mistake is to cover the cold applications with oiled silk, for, by preventing evaporation, it causes the dressings to get warm sooner, requiring fresh applications of cold, and these too frequent alternations of heat and cold irritate the parts and increase congestion. The antiphlogistic treatment described above, accompanied by a low diet and mild saline purgatives, will be found the best. Cold applications should be continued as long as they prove agreeable to the patient. In wounds of the joints, we have seen ice applied during six or eight weeks with the best result.

If these cold applications should not be tolerated any further by the patient, they ought to be replaced by poultices, or perhaps by warm water dressings. The latter, while they fulfil all the effects of a poultice, are preferable: they are easier removed, they are cleaner, and the patient can apply them himself, thus dispensing with the constant services of a nurse, an object of some importance in crowded wards. In wounds situated near the extremities of the forearm and legs, if the bones are much injured and many small splinters exist, then warm poultices or better still, warm water baths, will be found exceedingly beneficial. They relax the tension of the parts, promote the discharge of pus, and act favorably on the capillary vessels on the surface of the limb. For this purpose, tin boxes eight inches high, of the same width, and two feet long, having a lid, and an opening at the end for the reception of the limb, will answer very well. They are to be filled with warm water, which might be kept warm for a longer period by means of blankets.

3

Finally, an important point in the management of the wounds is a free discharge of pus, besides the protection of the limb from serous infiltration. For serous exudation, if allowed to collect, will soon be replaced by pus; whereas this will not be the case when a proper opening is made to facilitate the discharge of all fluids. The best proof hereof, is found in the treatment of the parts situated beneath the deep facia. If incisions be made early, when exudations are simply serous, the suppuration will be found to diminish ; but if incisions are not made early, extensive suppuration will follow, impeding the treatment, and endangering the life of the patient. This is especially true of gun-shot wounds. Sometimes a ball after striking a bone glances in a different direction, lacerating the muscles, and burrowing beneath the fascia, so that the finger cannot ascertain the direction of the ball. In such cases pus accumulates in these sinuses, as it cannot escape by the narrow and tortious opening made by the ball; this opening in fact becomes nearly closed by the swelling. In such cases, free incisions should be made at the entry and exit of the ball. By introducing the finger into the opening it can be used as a guide for the incisions, which should follow the long axis of the bone. Many modern surgeons are opposed to these dilatations of fresh wounds, except for the purpose of extracting foreign substances, or for ligating an artery.

Many therapeutical methods which have undergone discredit, though really efficacious, are slow in recovering their former position. Thus it is admitted that the dilatation of all gun-shot wounds is not necessary, but it would be a great mistake to assert that they are never necessary. Of course the surgeon has to decide whether an incision should be made or not. My experience, says Stromeyer, is undoubtedly such, that in cases where a ball has pursued a long and devious track, lacerating muscles and fascia before it, a dilatation is absolutely necessary to prevent the most frightful results. For extensive suppuration will soon take place, and in order to discharge the collection of pus, many incisions will be found necessary afterwards, when they might have been prevented by an early dilatation of the original opening. This principle is also applicable to gun-shot wounds in the thigh itself. When the laceration is in the neighborhood of the larger blood vessels, then the danger increases, because the inflammation might spread to the femoral vein, and thereby cause pyæmia; for this was observed in cases where the bone itself was not injured. Besides the dilatation of the wound, there are many important precepts which should be taken into consideration to prevent the secretion of wounds from accumulating. The wounded limb should be placed in such a manner that the discharge can leave the wound by the simple laws of gravity. An opening which is too small should be dilated; also, a fistulous track should be treated in the same manner, or a counter-opening made. Isolated abscesses should be opened as soon as fluctuation is felt. Sometimes it will be found necessary to apply leeches, or cut through the fascia, to avoid a fresh swelling. Young surgeons are generally very bold in making such incisions, but they forget that their object is the discharge of pus. Instead of putting the limb in an appropriate position, in order that pus may exude from the opening, they dress the wound with charpie and sticking plaster, besides a compress and a roller, and therefore no fluid can possibly escape. When such a bandage is removed after twenty-four hours, the pus escapes in great quantity. On discovering this, these surgeons are most anxious to get rid at once of all the pus and squeeze the limb most unmercifully, to the great distress of the patient. Heedless that the pus is formed as fast as it is removed, they reäpply their bandages, and of course the pus becomes more acrid and more fetid. As usual, this fault brings on another. They apply what is called an expulsive bandage, to prevent the accumulation of pus, but really it does nothing of the kind. When this fails they resort to solutions of nitrate of silver and chloride of soda, but still the pus continues to accumulate. Let our surgeons beware of such practice as this. One good incision in the right place, will diminish the quantity of the pus, change its quality, and improve the general health of the patient. By attention to these principles we shall avoid all deposits of pus, which are otherwise inevitable.

It is important for us to notice in this place that there are two different ways in which pus may accumulate near a gun-shot wound. The most common origin of pus deposits is when it fuses beneath the cellular tissue and reaches a spot different from its origin, this percolation taking place according to the laws of gravity. In the second instance, inflammation, swelling and fluctuation, show a local tendency to the formation of pus. Here, if early incisions are made, we shall find that nothing but serum, or a gelatinous fluid will be discharged, and yet these deposits of serum are connected with larger deposits which do contain pus. This can be proved sometimes by passing the finger through the smaller cavity into the larger one. It would appear that in such cases, the fluid portions of the pus becomes infiltrated in the tissues, and by their acrid nature cause a new inflammatory process, from which, in course of time, pus originates. After a few days, when poultices are applied, pus will appear in the new incisions, which become outlets of pus from the deeper cavities. In practice, it is important to discriminate between these two different sources of pus collections. The first kind should be opened as soon as they are discovered, the last kind may require the application of leeches to prevent the formation of abscesses.

After the expulsion of all foreign substances, and the separation of fragments of bone, the inflammatory symptoms decrease, and together with it the discharge of pus. At this period of the treatment, the limb should be rolled in flannel; flannel bandages should be used in preference to cotton. Pressure is necessary to diminish the œdematous swelling of the limb; but bandages should not be applied before a fracture has been consolidated, for otherwise the moving of the limb would counterbalance any benefit derived from the bandage. When wounds, which have ceased to secrete pus, become filled with granulations, in order to accelerate the healing process, they should be dressed with pieces of soft linen or cotton corresponding with the size of the wound, dipped in a solution of nitrate of silver, of one to five grains to the ounce of water, and the whole covered with a piece of oiled silk to prevent them from drying too quickly. All cerates and salves should be dispensed with. The only dressing used after the patient leaves the bed should consist of oiled charpie.

And now, while closing these general remarks on the treatment of gun-shot wounds affecting the shaft of bones, we would again particularly call the attention of our confreres to the necessity of keeping the patients on a low diet during the inflammatory state of the wound. The diet should correspond to the antiphlogistic treatment, and consist of light soups, a few vegetables, a small quantity of bread, and a cooling beverage, which treatment sometimes has to be continued for weeks.

GUN-SHOT WOUNDS AFFECTING THE ARTICULATIONS.

Wounds affecting the larger joints are generally so dangerous as to require an early operation. Their gravity and frequency, together with their manifold varieties make them peculiarly important for the consideration of the surgeon.

DIFFERENT KINDS OF INJURIES AFFECTING THE JOINTS.

A shot by simply grazing a joint may wound only the ligaments, without causing, however, any injury to the bone itself. On the other hand, if a ball strikes the end of a bone, it may, according to its force, either go through the bone or remain in it; or it may break off a portion of it, or, finally, if it has lost its power, it may strike the epiphysis and rebound, after causing more or less damage. In such cases, where the joint is

injured, the synovial capsule is not necessarily affected, but
generally fissures occur, which extend through the head of the
bone. The inflammation following this will sooner or late implicate the whole joint. Those wounds are the most dangerous
in which the extremity of the bone, together with the synovial
membrane have been torn and lacerated. The gravity of such
injuries is readily understood when we remember the liability
to inflammation of serous membranes in the first place, and
secondly, the extent of these membranes in the joints, together
with the various ligaments and tendons surrounding it, all of
which will become included in the process of inflammation; besides this, the danger is increased by the destruction of the
cartilaginous coverings of the bones, whereby the joint is destroyed. Moreover, the joints consisting of irregular cavities
will facilitate the accumulation of the secretions of the
wound, a condition which is much aggravated by the presence
of splinters and other foreign substances. The extremities of
bones are more spongy and vascular than other portions, consequently, when inflammation sets in, they offer a large surface
for suppuration. On examining such wounds soon after the
accident, the joint will be found to contain a large quantity of
blood together with lymph, immediately around the spot injured
by the passage of the ball. The medullary cavity itself show-
ing the extent of the injury. As soon as suppuration begins
in the wound, the extravasated blood will be decomposed, and
thereby rendered offensive. This condition will extend as far
as the fissures and embrace all the injured portion of bone.

PROGNOSIS OF INJURIES OF THE JOINTS.

In injuries of the larger joints, it commonly happens that
serous infiltration takes place around it. Inflammation sets in,
the limb begins to swell on both sides, the skin takes on a
bright red color, becomes hot and tense, and the epidermis
vesicated. The distal extremity of the limb becomes œdematous from obstruction of the venous circulation. Accompanying this condition, we find the following general symptoms: a frequent pulse, a dry tongue, constant thirst, and

from continued suffering, the patient frequently becomes delirious. The pain is increased by the slightest motion of the limb. Suppuration soon follows, generally preceded by a chill, and pyæmia, with all its sequela closes the scene. In these cases the pus is soon decomposed and fetid; gas forms in the cavity of the joint, and the patient becomes either comatose or delirious with an icteric hue, and death rapidly follows. Such are commonly the consequences of gun-shot wounds in the knee-joint. When these symptoms appear, amputation is no longer of any avail. An early operation only, would save the life of the patient. Should a smaller joint be injured, the symptoms which we have just enumerated are usually milder in proportion, and make their appearance more slowly. For instance, if the capsule of the joint should be slightly injured and no blood penetrate into the joint, the pus may still be normal; but if the pus so formed be retained within the capsule, it will cause extensive inflammation, and finally escape by a rupture of the capsule at its weakest point. The pus will then fuse into the cellular tissue between the muscles, cause phlegmonous inflammation and the formation of abscesses. It frequently happens in such cases that pus burrows the whole extent of the limb, so that if death does not take place from pyæmia, the profuse suppuration will so endanger the life of the patient, that amputation will be the last resort.

The symptoms which set in when the synovial capsule has not been injured, are very slow and gradual, though the joint may become implicated at last from the suppuration around it. When the extremity of a bone has been struck, so as to cause fissures through the epiphysis without injury to the cartilage, the cavity of the joint in such a case may not communicate with the wound; but in the process of suppuration, the cartilages become eroded, and pus will enter the cavity of the joint, causing intense inflammation at a late day, and the patient who had been previously considered in a favorable condition, will at once present all the dangerous symptoms above enumerated.

DIAGNOSIS OF INJURIES OF THE JOINTS.

From what we have already said, it will be found difficult to ascertain, in some cases, the true extent of the injury.
Doubtless, in many cases, the external appearance of the
wound will be a sufficient guide in diagnosis. A wound which
is considerably swollen, accompanied with much pain and high
fever, with fragments of bones, and an exposed cartilage,
while a bloody synovia oozes from the opening, can scarcely
allow us to doubt the nature of the injury. But there are many
cases, where it is very difficult to ascertain the extent of the
lesion. It is well known, that a ball striking a body in an
oblique manner, may glance off in a different direction, and
passing beneath the skin, may come out in a distant place
without penetrating the parts situated between the two open-
ings. This has been observed in the shoulder-, elbow-, and
knee-joint. But it is necessary to be cautious in concluding
from a superficial examination of such a wound. For it may
happen that the ball has entered the joint, while the limb was
in a different position from that in which it is examined. By
a change of position some muscle or tendon may obstruct
the entrance of the finger, and the discharge of synovia. It
is, therefore, very important to ascertain the exact position of
the limb when it received the shot, and to examine it in various positions. A swelling of the capsule of the joint, though
occurring imediately after the injury, is not a certain sign of
the joint being affected. For this may follow any lesion in the
neighborhood of the joint, and the capsule itself may be inflamed and distended without being touched by a ball.

TREATMENT OF INJURIES OF THE JOINTS.

It is well known that injuries of the joints when left alone
or neglected, speedily become dangerous, they therefore,
require more than all other wounds, the intervention of the
surgeon. In spite of the best and most energetic treatment,
the life of the patient is in jeopardy, and it therefore becomes
the imperative duty of the surgeon, either to amputate the
limb, or to resect the extremities of the bones, so as to

simplify the wound. In some cases it may be sufficient to make a free incision into the capsule of the joint, in order to give issue to the fluids which are there abundantly secreted. But the latter treatment is accompanied with long suffering, and followed by complete ankylosis of the joint. On the other hand, the process of healing is much more rapid after a resection, and frequently some mobility may be obtained in the limb.

Wounds of the wrist and ankle will heal under favorable conditions and a proper treatment, though they entail long suffering and a stiff joint. Amputation is necessary when the bones are badly crushed. Under these circumstances a resection is not advisable; the tendons being generally implicated at the same time that it is extremely difficult to avoid the numerous vessels and nerves which surround those joints: instead of resection, it is even preferable in such cases, to make a large opening into the articulation itself.

Wounds of the larger joints call for an immediate operation, unless the capsule alone be injured, and the bones not affected. In such a case, the wound may heal by a proper antiphlogistic treatment, though it will be followed by ankylosis of the joint. As an exception, and under very favorable circumstances, it may happen that wounds in which the bones have also been implicated, heal without an operation, but the life of the patient runs a great risk, and the responsibility of the surgeon is therefore very great.

Taking all things into consideration, we should say that in cases of injuries of the larger joints, complicated with the more or less damage of the bone, it is better to amputate, although under very favorable circumstances, resection may be tried. In the olden time, when a joint was lacerated, by a ball, amputation was invariably performed.

Larrey was the first to introduce resection into military surgery. But during the revolution in Paris, of 1848, we find that the most celebrated French surgeons performed no resections. In the late war of Schleswig-Holstein, out of forty cases of complicated gun-shot wounds in the elbow-joint, in which the whole joint was resected, thirty-two were discharged

4

cured, with preservation of the limb, and only six died. It can be proved that the resection of the elbow-joint at the least, is a less dangerous operation than amputation, or disarticulation, by comparing the lists of mortality of both operations. It must be considered also, that most of these resections were made under such circumstances, that the third part of the amputated cases died. This was certainly a great triumph for conservative surgery. When we consider how helpless a man becomes after losing an arm, we can realize the advantage of preserving such a limb, although a portion of its utility be lost. Wounds of the joints of the inferior extremities must be viewed in a different light. Thus, an artificial limb, or a wooden stump may be more serviceable than a crooked or stiff leg which cannot perform its natural functions. There is still another question connected with this subject, viz : the relative gravity of the two operations, a point still undecided. Resections of the hip and knee-joint did not give good results during the war of Schleswig-Holstein ; they should, however, still be tried, and perhaps would now give better results.

GUN-SHOT WOUNDS IN DIFFERENT BONES.

UPPER EXTREMITY.

INJURIES TO THE SHAFT OF THE HUMERUS.

The liability to splinter, which is characteristic of the humerus make its injuries very dangerous. If the soft parts are much lacerated, at the same time that the shaft of the bone has been splintered, amputation is at once necessary. But when the ball has only penetrated the muscles, without injuring the vessels and nerves, an attempt should be made to preserve the arm, though the bone be considerably crushed. The chief danger of these wounds, consists in the violent inflammation which generally sets in at the inner side of the biceps. This must be combated by venesection, leeches and iced applications. If much swelling takes place, incision will be found useful. There is great difficulty in maintaining the arm in a proper position. The best way to secure it is to bandage the fore-arm across the thorax, while the wounded part of the humerus is separated from the chest by a cushion filled with oat-chaff, and covered with oiled silk ; the fractured ends of the bone are then kept together by means of Scultet's bandage. The limb is to be supported on the outside by a pasteboard splint, the whole apparatus being secured by a roller bandage passed around it and the chest. Out of twenty-five cases of complicated wounds of the shaft of the humerus, which occurred during the above mentioned war, only four died, the others recovered perfectly ; though there were several instances in which the humerus had been broken into several fragments by grape-shot. In those cases no operation whatsoever was performed, nature alone accomplishing the cure. Consolidation took place sooner or later, and a useful limb was restored to the patient.

Injuries of the bone, in the neighborhood of the elbow, may

progress favorably if the fracture be a simple one. If the
humerus should be struck near its head, fissures when produced
will assume a downward direction, for the head being more
spongy and cellular, is not liable to such fissures. If the
ball should strike the bone lower down, such fissures may go
upwards and downwards. Stromeyer recommends, when these
fissures are very extensive, either to amputate at once, or if
amputation be not indicated, to trust to nature, and leave the
wound untouched. He thinks further, that when the removal
of the limb is absolutely necessary, amputation is preferable
to disarticulation.

INJURIES TO THE SHOULDER-JOINT.

Gun-shot wounds of the shoulder-joint are quite frequent, and
the injury may be done in every possible direction. The diagnosis of these injuries is sometimes difficult; at least to ascertain
the precise extent of the injury, for the joint being covered by
the whole thickness of the deltoid muscle, a thorough examination becomes almost impracticable when the deltoid is largely
developed. The ball may pass through a portion of this
muscle without touching the bone, or may even open the
capsule of the joint, without this fact being recognized until
the inflammation of the joint sets in. Fortunately, an exact
diagnosis between a mere flesh wound and an injury of the
capsule is not indispensable, the same antiphlogistic treatment
being applicable to both injuries. They generally heal with
stiffness of the joint.

When suppuration is so extensive as to endanger the life of
the patient, resection of the head of the humerus is evidently
indicated. Not that resection is absolutely necessary in fractures of the head of the humerus, for such wounds may heal
after the splinters have been extracted, though this occurs at
the expense of a stiff joint. In these cases, if resection is
performed, a better result will be obtained, because some
mobility generally follows. This operation may be performed
at once or after suppuration has taken place.

The resection of this joint, says Esmarch, has given us such

good results and so rapidly, that if we add to this the benefit
of an artificial joint instead of an ankylosed limb, we can
not hesitate to declare that *resection should be performed at
once in all injuries of the shoulder-joint, in which the head of the
humerus is fractured from gun-shot wounds.*

The rule which we have just given is based upon the following statistics: eight cases were left to the curative efforts of
nature; of these five died, and in one it was yet undecided
after six months' treatment whether an operation would not
still be required. Out of nineteen cases, where resection of
the head of the humerus was performed, only seven died, and
twelve recovered perfectly, with a more or less useful limb.
In none of these cases did ankylosis take place. Some were
healed in less than three months. Among those cases which
proved fatal, some had been operated during the inflammatory
stage, others were treated in unhealthy places, where the
simplest wounds gave rise to pyæmia.

Larrey and Guthrie have established the rule, that resection
should only be performed in those cases where only the
head of the humerus is injured; but if the injury extends as
far as the medulla, the limb should be taken off at the joint.

The statements of Stromeyer and Esmarch are opposed to
this. During the Schleswig-Holstein campaign, most of the
resections included a portion of the shaft of the bone, sometimes as much as four and five inches. If the ball, after
fracturing the head of the humerus, should have entered the
chest, it may still be advisable to operate, provided there is a
chance of saving the patient's life; the resulting loss of blood
would be more serviceable than otherwise.

We shall now give those methods of resection which we
think the best.

Method of Langenbeck.—A longitudinal incision is made in
front of the joint, beginning at the anterior edge of the
acromion, extending from two to four inches in the direction of
the tendon of the long head of the biceps, which is reached
after the skin and deltoid muscle have been divided. The
sheath of the tendon should now be opened on its outside, the

knife being passed closely to the inner edge of the greater tuberosity of the humerus; after the tendon has been exposed, it
can be recognized by its silvery hue; the knife should then be
introduced into the joint, the point being carried forward and
the back resting against the bone. The capsule being opened,
the cartilage of the head will be seen beneath the anterior
edge of the acromion. The tendon of the biceps should now
be taken out of the bicipital groove by means of a blunt hook,
drawn inwards and held by an assistant (the edges of the wound
during this time being separated by hooks). The assistant who
holds the arm should now rotate the limb inwards, by which the
larger tuberosity comes into view. A circular incision should
then be directed around this tuberosity, beginning at the
opening of the capsule, and ending at the external edge of the
bicipital groove, the convexity of the cut being outwards.
By this incision, the tendon of the supraspinatus, infraspinatus
and teres major will be divided. The arm is now rotated
outwards, in order to bring the lesser tuberosity in front, and
the tendon of the biceps should be replaced in the groove. A
semi-lunar incision will then be carried around the lesser
tuberosity, by which the tendon of the subscapularis muscle
is divided. By means of these incisions, which have the
form of the Greek letter Φ, the capsule, together with all the
tendons and ligaments, will be divided down to the bone; so
that the head of the humerus can now be pushed out, the
tendon of the biceps being again drawn inwards by means of
a hook. The head of the bone should be pushed out of its
socket and made to project out of the wound, at which
time the operator introduces a blunt-pointed knife behind
the head of the bone, dividing the posterior part of the
capsule and separating the pectoralis major, latissimus, dorsi
and teres major as low down as the saw must be applied.
This is done by carrying the elbow backwards and upwards,
so that the upper end of the humerus projects out of the
wound. After the head of the bone has been removed, the
arm should be bandaged in the manner above described, the
greater part of the incision being brought together by sutures.

This method is of easy execution, when the head of the humerus is not completely separated from the bone by the force of the ball; but if this should be the case, then another incision, two inches long, should meet the upper part of the first incision at right angles, cutting across a portion of the deltoid muscle near the acromion. By this means a sufficient space will be had to remove the head of the bone or its fragments. The objections to this method is the difficulty of obtaining of a free discharge of the secreted fluids from the wound.

Method of Stromeyer.—The following method was proposed by Stromeyer and performed with the best results. A semi-lunar cut beginning at the posterior edge of the acromion, should be directed downwards three inches towards the outer side of the humerus, the convexity of this incision being outward. In this manner the joint will be opened from above and behind. The arm should then be drawn forwards and upwards, thereby exposing the anterior portion of the capsule together with the tendons and ligaments, all of which should be divided with the exception of the long tendon of the biceps By this method, the secretions of the wound are easily discharged while the patient lies on his back. No infiltration of pus can occur, and the results have proved the excellence of the process. Patients have recovered in half the time required by the other methods, where the secretions are not so easily removed. The greater part of the incision should be sewed up, and only a portion left open for the drainage of the wound. The arm should be flexed at right angles and bandaged to the body. The wound itself should be dressed with cold water applications. When suppuration takes place and the pus looks healthy, warm water dressings may be substituted, and finally it may be covered with oiled charpie. The cavity will soon fill up with granulations. The arm should not be moved during the suppurative stage. The wound can be syringed with warm water to keep it clean. When the wound begins to cicatrize, the limb should be moved gently and gradually until mobility is established.

As we have already stated, out of nineteen resections of the
shoulder joint, made during the three years' campaign in
Schleswig-Holstein, seven cases only died, all of which suc-
cumbed from pyæmia. The post-mortem examination of all
these cases revealed either the decomposition of the medullary
portion of the bone, or phlebitis of the axillary vein, and
sometimes both together.

The length of time which intervened, says Esmarch, between
the wound and the operation, seemed to exercise some influence
upon the result; thus out of six cases operated upon in the first
twenty-four hours after the injury, two died. In three cases, resection was performed while inflammation was at its height, on
the third and fourth days; of these, two proved fatal. Secondary
resections were performed in ten cases after suppuration had
existed for some time; of these, three died. Some of the latter,
however, would have been saved, had the operation been performed earlier, say in the first twenty-four hours. We should
therefore state the rule, either to operate at once, or postpone
it until suppuration has been fully established. During this
time the antiphlogistic treatment will prepare them for the
subsequent operation. Another remarkable result observed in
those resections was that the mortality from resection of the
left arm was greater, as compared to that of the right arm, an
observation which was also made in resections of the elbow.

INJURIES OF THE ELBOW.

Gun-shot wounds of the elbow are comparatively more
dangerous than those of the shoulder. Instances where recovery took place after serious injuries of the bones, are very
rare. It is therefore laid down as a rule in military surgery,
in all cases where the joint is implicated, that the limb must be
sacrificed in order to save the life of the patient. But in later
times, resections of the elbow-joint have been performed where
amputation would have taken place previously. Langenbeck
and Stromeyer are entitled to the credit of establishing this
conquest of conservative surgery. Larrey never performed it,
Guthrie mentioned it but never executed it himself, and the

military reports up to the year of 1848-9 show that this operation had not been performed during the revolutionary epoch in Paris or Italy, in Berlin or Hungary. During the war of Schleswig-Holstein, the principal injuries which occurred to the elbwow-joint were as follows : In most cases the ball had struck the ulna, while the soldier was either loading or firing his gun, the arm being in a bent position. Sometimes the ball entered the soft parts of the forearm, went some distance along the muscles, crushing the radius or ulna. In very few cases the condyles of the humerus were injured, a fact which can only be explained by the position of the humerus, being protected by the radius and ulna when the arm is flexed on the forearm.

" In all cases, says Stromeyer, when I diagnosed an injury of the bones of the elbow, I did not hesitate to perform resection at once. The joint was opened from behind by an incision at the inner side of the olecranon. A second incision was then made perpendicular to the first, opening the joint from the head of the radius to the *external* condyle. This incision should extend over the olecranon and divide the tendon of the triceps. After the joint has been opened on the posterior portion, exposing fully the articulation, all the loose fragments of bone should be extracted; even those which are still in connection should be taken out with the knife or bone forceps, the ulnar nerve being, however, carefully respected. If the ulna was alone injured, the end of it should be sawed off, with a corresponding portion of the radius. Of the' latter, however, no more than the head and neck should be taken off, though the fissures of the other bone, the ulna, might have extended further down. In such cases to have removed all the injured portions of the bone, would have caused the sacrifice of three or four inches, an operation which would be more complicated and less advantageous; for, even if the patient recovered and the limb was preserved, we should not have had either an artificial joint or ankylosis. I have never had cause to regret having acted in this cautious manner, but on the contrary, have observed that a new bone was established from that

5

part of the ulna, which otherwise would have been sacrificed. When the radius was fractured below the neck, the fragments were extracted, the ends being smoothed off with a saw. In such a case the olcranon alone was removed from the adjoining bone, as this would otherwise project after the healing of the wound, and cause much annoyance."

The ulna being the bone upon which the solidity of the joint chiefly depends, it should be preserved as much as possible. After removing the fractured portions from the ulna and radius, and sawing the ends of these bones, it may be neces- sary to saw off likewise a portion of the trochlea humeri. In many cases the bone need not be touched at all, it being sufficient to pare off the cartilage with the knife; a process which did not interfere with the healing of the wound.

When the adjoining part of the humerus is also injured, the operation is somewhat difficult. Generally one of the two condyles will be crushed, and the fissure extends beyond the capsular ligament. To resect in such a case, all the fissured portion, would involve a loss of some two and a half inches of bone. It is, in fact, only necessary to resect a small portion of the injured bone, but then the olecranon process of the ulna must be removed at the same time. In dressing the wound, the upper portion should be brought together by means of sutures, and the lower portion left open for the discharge of the secretions.

The statistics of this operation are exceedingly favorable. Whilst under the same circumstances most of the amputated cases died, most of the resected cased recovered perfectly and retained the mobility of the hand, though there was generally partial ankylosis of the elbow.

There are, undoubtedly, cases where amputation instead of resection must be performed. For instance, when the ball, besides shattering the bone, has likewise torn the main vessels at the inner side of the arm, causing bloody infiltration of the forearm and secondary hemorrhage, then the brachial artery must necessarily be tied, and this would cause mortification of the forearm, as the collateral vessels which usually keep up the circulation could scarcely be avoided in performing resection of the joint. Amputation is furthermore indicated when the soft parts around the joint are extensively lacerated.

We find the following statistical results obtained during the campaign of Schleswig-Holstein: out of fifty-four cases of amputation of the humerus, nineteen died; out of forty cases of resections of the elbow, only six died. On the other hand, the wound after resection heals more slowly than after amputation; but when we consider that the limb is preserved, the advantage of the two operations can scarcely be weighed in the same balance. It is a strange fact that the healing process is much shorter, the more we have to sacrifice of the ligaments and capsule of the joint.

As to the treatment of a resected joint, rest and a comfortable position are the main objects to be attended to. Immediately after the operation, the limb should be placed on a wooden concave splint, padded with cotton wadding, covered with oiled silk, to prevent it from being soiled. The splint should reach from the upper third of the humerus downwards to the ends of the fingers, and should be bent at the elbow at an angle of 140°; care being taken at the same time, that no undue pressure be exercised on the internal condyles. For this purpose an opening should be made into the splint. The arm resting in this way on the excavated splint should be placed on a large cushion filled with chopped straw and fastened in this position. The wound itself must be dressed with cold water applications, and when suppuration is established, with warm water. When the suppuration ceases, oiled charpie should be used to cover the wound.

It is of the utmost importance that the arm be moved from the splint. A sufficient quantity of charpie should be stuffed on both sides of the arm, in order to absorb the secretions of the wound. This can be replaced when soiled, without moving the arm. If pus collects in the tissues, it is not proper to press or syringe the wound, it being preferable to remove the pus by a new incision. After the wound has progressed so far as to become filled by granulations, the limb may be cautiously raised and bandaged with flannel. At this period warm water baths of the whole arm will prove very serviceable, to reëstablish the mobility of hand and fingers.

It is a well known fact, that artificial joints, can only be produced by motion; it is, therefore, important to make an early attempt to establish the joint. We may begin to move the arm cautiously before the wound has completely closed. But if this should irritate the wound, giving the granulations a livid appearance, we should stop the manipulations; for otherwise inflammation and hæmorrhage might ensue. As soon as the wound has completely healed, we must advise the patient to move his arm frequently; but this being painful and therefore commonly neglected by the patient, it must be done by the nurse or some other attendant. When ankylosis takes place, it is generally to be attributed to negligence in this respect. The importance of these precepts in regard to the after-treatment, says Esmarch, was clearly proved in those cases which happened to fall into the hands of the Danes, after resection had been performed. The Danish surgeons never performed this operation, and therefore had no idea of the importance of motion to the resected limb. When those prisoners were exchanged, they therefore returned with ankylosed joints. It was observed also that the ankylosed limbs were bent at an angle of 130° to 140°, which was the position when the arm was treated. This degree of flexion was chosen because it seemed to give the patient less pain than any other position, and in case of partial ankylosis rendered the limb more useful.

It has been observed that mobility of the joint is not dependant upon the extent of resected surface; for it happened that in some cases ankylosis took place where a large portion of the bones was removed, while others recovered with a comparatively useful limb, though a small portion of the bone had been taken off.

INJURIES OF THE FOREARM.

An injury of one or both bones of the forearm, from a gunshot, seldom requires amputation when there are no complica-

tions to endanger the life of the patient. Extensive inflamma.
tion of both bones may be controlled by leeching and cold
applications. The treatment of such cases is simple : the
forearm should be placed on a splint, extending from the elbow
to the end of the fingers. All tight bandages should be carefully avoided. In the beginning, iced applications should be
made; and afterwards, warm fomentations. The splinters
must be extracted when detached by the suppurative process.
At a later period, flannel bandages are of a great benefit.
Forty cases of injuries of the forearm are reported. In six of
these both bones were fractured; in sixteen cases the radius,
and in eighteen cases the ulna alone were injured. All recovered.

INJURIES OF THE WRIST.

Gun-shot wounds of the wrist are very dangerous on account
of the inflammation which generally follows such injuries.
They frequently affect the whole system, and show a great
tendency to pyæmia. This can be explained by the numerous
tendons which cover this joint, retained in their positions by
the annular ligament. When inflammation is developed in
this region, pus collects beneath these ligaments, causing
pressures on the nerves and producing intense pain. Moreover,
suppuration of the medullary portion of the bone generally
takes place, embracing the chances of pyæmia, and then amputation itself is of no avail. When the swelling is not very
extensive, an energetic antiphlogistic treatment must be
adopted; iced applications, leeches, and even venesection,
together with small doses of opium must be resorted to.
Incisions may be made to relieve the swelling and pain. If
the soft parts around the wrist are much lacerated, an early
amputation is required.

INJURIES OF THE HAND.

Injuries of the second series of the carpi and metacarpi,
together with the phalanges, are not so dangerous as injuries
of the first row of bones of the hand, and do not absolutely

require an operation. The expectant method should be followed here. No operation at least is justified when the wounded were not treated immediately after the injury. Suppuration sets in at an early period, and as long as the acute stage continues, the surgeon should not interfere with the wound. Wounds of the fingers occur very frequently in battle. When disarticulation or amputation are performed at an early day, no serious symptoms are found to rise. But it was observed during the late campaign of Schleswig-Holstein, that all operations performed upon the fingers forty-eight hours after the injury occurred, only increased the inflammation, caused suppuration in the course of the tendons, and occasioned stiffness of one or more fingers, if not the whole hand. During the campaign, says Stromeyer, I never performed disarticulation of a finger, except immediately after the injury was received. I have never observed tetanus supervene after these wounds. The beneficial effects of venesection are abundantly proved by many instances.

All injuries of the hand should be treated by placing the extremity on a board adapted for that purpose. Poultices are useful when suppuration has commenced, and more so than in all other wounds of the upper extremities; they also will be required for a longer period.

LOWER EXTREMITY.

INJURIES TO THE SHAFT OF THE FEMUR.

The simplest and least dangerous accident that can happen this bone from a gun-shot wound, is, that the ball should fracture the bone without much crushing or splintering. An accurate examination of these wounds is often difficult, especially when the limb is already much swollen. If the bone be fractured by a large projectile, and the soft parts extensively lacerated, then all idea of preserving the limb should be aban-

doned, and the sooner amputation is performed the better for
the patient. The gravity of the injury increases in proportion
as the wound is nearer the trunk; inflammation, suppuration
and phlebitis being more likely to occur in a short and moveable fragment, than in a longer one. Instead of the plastic
exudation which takes place around the ends of bone in simple
fractures, in these cases the fragments are exposed to suppuration, followed by necrosis; so that the possibility of union by
the formation of callus is destroyed. The provisional callus is
sometimes formed, however, around the necrosed fragments,
and partial consolidation takes place. Then the suppuration
diminishes though it will not disappear until the sequestra are
expelled. When left to the slow efforts of nature, this may
require years for its completion. All these reasons should
decide the military surgeon in favor of immediate amputation,
at least in the great majority of such cases. Such, at all
events is the present state of military surgery. Nevertheless,
the question arises whether it would not be proper to attempt
to save the limb under favorable circumstances. Experience
has proved that this can only be done when the treatment is
commenced at once, without any transportation of the patient. No bandage however carefully adjusted, can obviate
the injury caused by transportation; and when we take into
consideration the rude wagons commonly used to convey the
wounded, it becomes evident no subsequent care could neu-
tralize the damage so caused. It is much better to convey
such wounded patients to some house near the battle-field, and
incur the risk of falling into the enemy's hands, than to trans-
port them. The dictates of humanity, the precepts of science,
command that such cases should be sacred alike to friend and
foe. If, therefore, the surgeon expects or undertakes to save
the limb, the first care is to place it in a proper position.
Unless the swelling be already too extensive, the fractured
ends of bone should be adjusted, while the patient is under the
influence of chloroform. Long cushions filled with oat-chaff
should be placed on both sides of the limb, and extension
maintained by wooden splints resting on these, this being

secured by some appropriate bandage. The whole apparatus should be so disposed, that an easy access to the wound can be had. A strict antiphlogistic treatment is absolutely required. All probing and otherwise irritating the wound under pretence of searching for foreign bodies, should not be practiced. The wound should be dressed with care and delicacy, and it is quite unsurgical to press the wound or raise the limb. As soon as the inflammatory stage has gone by, Scultet's bandage can be used with good advantage and the splints applied more closely. In case the patient suffers from the limb being placed in a straight position, a double inclined plane will be found very useful. Of course the surgeon should endeavor, as much as possible, to retain the normal length of the limb. But when suppuration is too profuse and long continued, threatening the life of the patient, then, says Stromeyer, it is well enough to save the limb, even at the expense of some shortening. By allowing the muscles to contract naturally, the healthy portions of bone will overlap each other, and becoming readily united, suppuration will soon cease. This distinguished author says, that within eight days, he has observed the most decided advantage following this plan of treatment. In such cases, the limb should be placed on a double inclined plane, great care being taken to maintain it in its proper position by means of the foot-board.

The great trochanter is sometimes splintered without a complete fracture of the femur, an accident which is sometimes very dangerous on account of the spongy nature of this part of the bone. An antiphlogistic treatment should be instituted, and free incision be made when it is necessary to get rid of the pus. It is dangerous to attempt to remove splinters at an early period, for it is well known that access of air, which is thereby occasioned, is very prejudicial to the wound, generally causing suppuration and inflammation of the joint.

INJURIES OF THE HIP JOINT.

Gun-shot wounds of the hip-joint are almost always fatal, partly on account of the complications which generally exist, and partly on account of the tendency of such wounds to pyæmia. Fortunately this injury seldom occurs. Larrey, who undoubtedly had the greatest experience of any military surgeon up to the present time, says in his surgical clinick, that he never saw a case of the kind. This can be explained by the fact that a wound affecting the hip-joint generally extends to the contents of the pelvis, and therefore proves rapidly fatal; moreover, post-mortem examinations are seldom made after important battles, and no means exist of ascertaining the proportion of the different wounds.

The diagnosis of these injuries is difficult, from the fact of their being deeply situated and covered by several thick and powerful muscles, interfering with an accurate examination. The great swelling which rapidly takes place, the acute pain occasioned by motion of the limb, are the only symptoms which can lead us to infer, that the joint is implicated.

Injuries of the neck of the bone, or in the neighborhood of the great trochanter, are not so rare, though quite as difficult to diagnose as injuries of the joint. The characteristic symptoms of fracture of the neck are not apparent at first. Several such cases have been observed that were not recognized before the symptoms of pyæmia set in. Without surgical intervention such cases ended fatally, on account of the fissures which generally extended to the head of the femur, so that when suppuration took place, pus was transmitted to the capsule of the joint, causing inflammation of the hip-joint and all its sequela.

When the trochanters are injured, they are predisposed to suppuration on account of their spongy nature, and this soon extends to the medullary portion of the bone, whence pus will be taken up by the veins and carried throughout the system. Surgical intervention being necessary, the choice is between disarticulation or resection. During the war of Schleswig-Holstein, disarticulation of the femur was performed seven times, five of which were by-Langenbeck; of these one survived, a young man aged seventeen years. This unfortunate result induced Stromeyer to try resection in the following case, which we relate as highly instructive.

At the battle of Kolding, on the 23d of April, 1849; a Danish
musketeer received a ball which fractured the left femur,
passing in an oblique direction through both trochanters. The
local and general symptoms appeared so favorable at first, that
it was thought likely to heal without any operation. The patient
was placed in a proper position and treated on the antiphlogistic plan. Nevertheless, extensive suppuration took place,
the pus becoming decomposed and offensive. An incision
was made through the wound, to allow the free discharge of
pus, and to remove any splinters that might be detached.
This incision extended upwards, four inches above the gun-shot
wound, and the same distance below it; a few terse fragments
were then extracted. On further examination it was found
that a fissure extended through the neck of the femur, extending to the capsule ; the upper portion of the fractured bone
was then seized by means of a strong hooked forceps, and the
capsule and ligamentum teres were cut with a scalpel, so that
the head of the bone was thus disarticulated. The lower end
of the femur was next pushed out of the wound, and all the
injured portion, two inches long, sawed off below the lesser
trochanter. The operation was not a difficult one, and the
condition of the patient improved during the first two days
after the operation. There was less fever, and some hope was
entertained of saving the life of the patient. Nevertheless,
on the third day a chill announced the dreaded symptoms of
purulent absorption ; a secondary abscess was formed on the
right shoulder, and in the foot ; the patient died on the 20th
of May. At the post-mortem examination, it was found that
the tuberosity of the ischium was injured, and that the
medullary portion of that bone was infiltrated with decomposed pus. The foot and shoulder-joints on the right side
were also filled with pus.

There is no doubt that resection is a less dangerous operation than disarticulation. We would, therefore, advise resection as a preferable operation in all cases, where no laceration
of the anterior side of the femur has taken place, the vessels
and nerves being at the same time uninjured. The best time

for this operation is after the suppurative process has commenced, for by this means we give him all the chances of life and lessen the dangers of pyæmia.

INJURIES OF THE KNEE-JOINT.

The dangers which we have already stated as usually accompanying injuries of the joints, reach their maximum in those of the knee-joint. The injury may be situated in the synovial capsule alone, or it may implicate the bone likewise. The former kind are rare, and yet the inflammation and suppuration which follow, generally require amputation of the thigh at a later period, though much could be done by an antiphlogistic treatment to diminish the inflammation and allow the wound to heal. There are few cases on record who have recovered under this method. It must be borne in mind, that though the wound may heal externally, and consequently no synovia be discharged, still chronic inflammation of the synovial membrane may exist, causing the wound to reöpen, so that an amputation of the thigh will become necessary. The fear of ankylosis should not therefore prompt us to attempt too early a motion of the limb. Most of the injuries of the knee-joint implicate the bones more or less. It is important, though difficult, to make a diagnosis of the extent and seat of injury. When the bones are extensively fractured, the intense swelling and pain of the knee-joint will hardly allow a mistake on the subject, though the finger cannot reach the full extent of the wound.

We would therefore formulate the following proposition : *All gun-shot wounds of the knee-joint in which the condyles of the femur or tibia are injured require immediate amputation of the thigh.* This sad truth, long stated by the old authorities, is unfortunately still true at the present time. Esmarch says, that, regretting to sacrifice a limb for an apparently trifling wound, he was often prompted by pity to attempt its preservation, but as often did he repent the trial. The symptoms of purulent infection set in so quickly that medical intervention proved of no avail; and even when a powerful antiphlogistic

treatment diminished inflammation, and apparently gave hope
of a favorable prognosis, yet amputation had to be performed
at a later period, and then with little chance of preserving the
patient's life. This statement is fully confirmed by Guthrie, in
his treatise of gun-shot wounds of the extremities. He says,
that wounds of the knee-joint, when one or both epiphyses are
fractured, require immediate amputation : he states that he
never saw a case recover without it, and that if there is only
a slight injury of the patella, the cure may be tried without
amputation, but not so if the synovial capsule has been
touched. For though the wound will probably heal, amputation will become necessary at a later period. He recommends
an active antiphlogistic treatment as absolutely necessary, and
deprecates warm poultices as the infallible precursors of amputation.

During the campaign of Schleswig-Holstein, the results of
amputation of the thigh were so unfavorable, that it was
always reluctantly performed. Out of one hundred and
twenty-eight cases, seventy-seven died, and only fifty-one
recovered. Many of the cases which proved fatal had been
amputated after infiltration and suppuration had already taken
place.

If the shaft of the femur or tibia has been struck some
distance from the joint, it is at times impossible to say
whether the joint be implicated or not. In younger individuals
at least, hope may be entertained that fissures have not progressed so far as the head of the bone; such cases recover
without any inflammation or stiffness of the joint.

INJURIES OF THE LEG.

Although one or both bones of the leg may be injured, the
limb should be preserved, unless hemorrhage or other complications make amputation necessary. A ball may pass through
the head of the tibia without splintering the bone. If the
ball should be lodged in this part of the tibia it should be
extracted, either by enlarging the opening or by means of the
gouge. If the tibia be struck at its middle or lower portion,

the ball passing through, the bone is generally much splintered. In these cases extensive suppuration is apt to follow, and therefore the danger of purulent absorbtion will influence our prognosis. In the campaign of Schleswig-Holstein a partial resection of the tibia for the purpose of removing the splinters, was scarcely better than the expectant treatment, and commonly resulted in pyæmia. Stromeyer says that in those cases where the tibia was much damaged, he preferred to amputate, even though the fibula was not injured. He states further, that having frequently seen pyæmia follow amputation likewise, he does not feel authorized to pass a final judgment on the subject. It must be taken into consideration also, that many of those cases did not come under his care until twenty-four hours after the accident. It is evident that where the circumstances of the amputation would be more favorable, the results would be correspondingly modified.

We need scarcely say, that when both bones of a leg are crushed, amputation will generally be required.

If the fibula only be injured, the wound need not be considered dangerous, and nature will generally remove the splinters.

The apparatus for the treatment of gun-shot wounds of the leg, consists of the fracture box we have already described ; into this the limb should be placed when both bones are fractured : a paste-board splint will be sufficient when the fibula alone is injured.

When the malleoli are struck by grazing shots, amputation will not be required, though such wounds generally heal with ankylosis of the tibio-tarsal articulation. Should the lower end of the tibia be much crushed by a ball, amputation is certainly indicated.

INJURIES OF THE FOOT.

The most dangerous wounds of the foot are caused by bombshells. Stromeyer says, that they frequently become gangrenous, followed by prostration of the system, and sometimes tetanus. Injuries from musket-balls are not so dangerous, and under favorable circumstances generally recover. The treatment consists of iced applications, leeches, and saline purgatives, otherwise, the same treatment may applied as that described, for injuries of the hand.

GUN-SHOT WOUNDS OF THE BODY.

Injuries affecting the head and trunk seldom require surgical methods, other than the general antiphlogistic treatment.

In gun-shot wounds of the *lower maxillary bone*, no splinters should be removed except those which are entirely loose, leaving the other fragments to be afterwards separated by the suppurative process. It will be observed that in most cases of injuries of the lower maxillary, however extensive they may be, union will take place after the removal of a large portion of the bone by the suppurative process; for the periosteum being retained, a new formation of bone will take place. Resection, therefore, may be considered bad surgery. Bandaging is also unnecessary; the chief care consists in keeping the mouth clean, which can be done by syringing it with cold and later with warm water. This is important in order to obviate the irritative properties of pus, which when swallowed, cause disorder of the stomach and bowels.

The *clavicule* more than any other bone, demonstrates the advantage of the expectant method of treatment : there any operation, whatsoever, at the begining is useless, if not dangerous.

Injuries of the *scapula* only prove fatal, if the fracture extends to the joint. In such cases, the wound never should be dilated, and no fragments ought to be extracted until it has been ascertained that the joint is not implicated.

CONCLUSION.

Our task is finished. We have prepared it with the zeal which a good cause deserves, and we now send it forth on its own merits. The rules which we have laid down in the foregoing pages, are derived from the experience gathered in the campaign of Schleswig-Holstein. Though some surgical reports of the late war in the Crimea, and Italy, are sometimes at variance with these precepts, we think, nevertheless, they will stand the test of time and true science.

And now, Confrères, Surgeons of the army of the South! we have dedicated this pamphlet to you, and sincerely trust that it may be a safe guide on the battle-field, in the ambulance, and in the hospital. Should it be the means of saving one human life, or, even one useful limb, our labor will not have been in vain.

M. SCHUPPERT.